The Too Busy Trap
2nd Edition

Too busy is a refuge: it's a safe place to hide when doing the right thing becomes too uncomfortable.

Other Hollin Books:

GU00707615

Power Coaching

The Steps Before Step One

How To Empty The Too Hard Box

Ideas For Wimps

Behavioural Scorecards

How To Escape From Cloud Cuckoo Land

Behavioural Coaching 2nd Edition

Behavioural Safety for Leaders

Notes on Behavioural Management Techniques 3rd Edition

Many thanks to everyone who read the drafts and sent me comments and suggestions, each of whom changed the plot in some way. Many thanks to Ryan, Manny, Bruce, Craig, Andy, Rachel, Joanne, Lisa and Nicola. Thanks to Dave and Claire for appearing on the cover and taking the photos. Extra thanks to Lynn Dunlop for the meticulous editing of this latest edition of the booklet.

Special thanks to Joanne for the fabulous, insightful cartoons.

Hollin Ltd
Westminster House
10 Westminster Road
Macclesfield
Cheshire
SK10 1BX
howard@hollin.co.uk

First edition published by Hollin Publishing Nov 2011
Second edition published by Hollin Publishing July 2017
Hollin Publishing is a division of Hollin Consulting Ltd
© Copyright 2017 Hollin Consulting Ltd
978-0-9575211-3-1

Foreword to the first edition

By Ryan Olson

Some time ago I flew to the UK to do some work with Howard for a client that had a scary safety record. They needed help, and the big boss needed to be paying attention to the problem. At our first meeting with the leadership team, guess who was missing: The big boss was *too busy* to see me after paying for my plane ticket across the Atlantic. Later, as Howard and I reflected together on the lack of safety leadership at the site, he said to me, "Clearly, being *too busy* is NOT an effective strategy."

That comment stuck. It's also literally stuck to the left hand speaker of my desktop computer at the office. Since hearing it, the credo has inspired me to say no to things, put important stuff first and less important stuff last, delete dumb stuff from my life, and find clever ways to take better charge of my environment.

Not surprisingly, like most antecedents, the sticky note hasn't solved all my *too busy* problems. In this book Howard writes about the difficulty of "stepping out of the ongoing stream of activity" in order to get a proper perspective on what you are doing. Recently I was swept away by the white-water. I was just reacting to stuff (and over-reacting). I was stressed and anxious, and had trouble sleeping. I know my wife and daughter did not enjoy this period, and the people I led at work probably felt uneasy and alone. Being *too busy* is a special kind of misery for the person who is stuck in it, and for the people who have to deal with a person who is overwhelmed.

If you aren't on your toes, your workplace will pull you into the *too busy* trap. Everyone is vulnerable – did I mention I specialize in self-management research? I work hard to get my environment right so I am on my best behaviour. However, during the worst of my crisis, I felt like a total victim. I felt almost righteous in my victim-hood, because I was *too busy* after winning several new projects. Now with some perspective, and especially after reading Howard's book, I can see lots of missed opportunities for keeping my life under control so I could actually enjoy the new and exciting work.

Are you currently feeling overwhelmed with your job or family life? Do you work with someone who deflects work, or makes excuses for sloppy behaviour, with the *too busy* excuse? Throw a rope ashore, pull yourself out of the stream of busyness, and pause to read this book and reflect. It's a short read, so even if you're *too busy* you can do it. It is loaded with simple ideas for shaking up the status quo and taking more control of your life.

You can easily track how you spend your time (and with whom); map your high-activity, but low-value tasks; provide better social consequences for *too busy* bosses or office bullies; working one day a week from home; and more. You owe it to yourself to prove that, in Howard's words, you can "manage yourself out of a paper bag."

Ryan Olson PhD
Portland
Oregon

Foreword to the second edition
Manuel Rodriguez

I admit it, I have been caught in the *too busy* trap. I have also worked with too many bosses who are *too busy*. A former boss and mentor of mine used to come into my office daily and ask, "Manny, are you productive or busy?" Every day he would ask me, and unfortunately most days I was *too busy* to even realize the sheer brilliance of his words encouraging me to be productive instead of busy.

There is a clear distinction between one who is productive versus one who is just *too busy*. Time management is critical. Evaluating your own behaviours - 'what' you are doing and 'why' you are doing these things - is vital. The ability to focus on the important stuff is a clear differentiator between those who are productive and successful, versus those who are *too busy*. Finally, looking at your workplace environment, as Howard points out time and again in the book, can lead to long lasting productive work habits.

Howard provides context to individuals suffering from being *too busy* or who work with those who are *too busy*. After reading the book again myself, I recognized that I was assuming a *too busy* state to avoid certain tasks, focusing on low value/low effort tasks instead of high value/low effort; the "money" as Howard explains. I also evaluated my day-to-day, week-to-week activities, to see exactly how I was spending my *too busy* days. A range of activities prevailed such as low value meetings, the email battle, and being distracted by my boss rather than doing work that actually brought in value to my team, my clients and the organization as a whole. I realized quickly that I frequently fall into many of the motivational traps Howard describes, and honestly I was sick of it all and wanted to be productive, not *too busy*.

Today I find myself more productive than busy (most days anyway). I recognize both my behaviours and the environment will support productivity if I set myself up right. For example, I wrote this foreword while on a plane from Orlando to Los Angeles. I used the time to be productive in the work I enjoy doing. I wrote this foreword for Howard and I started working on a strategic plan for a new business venture. When I landed, I got to enjoy the rest of my day rather than worry about task completion in the evening or some other day if I didn't get caught being *too busy*.

I admit to getting caught in the *too busy* trap. The first step is clear: Own it, then do something about it. Howard provides some great context in looking at your environment, your behaviour, and strategies to become productive versus busy.

Manuel "Manny" Rodriguez, M.S.
Vice President, ABA Technologies, Inc.
Executive Director, OBM Network
Melbourne, Florida
U.S.A.

> *"My favorite things in life don't cost any money. It's really clear that the most precious resource we all have is time."*
> Steve Jobs

Contents

1. Introduction

Here are some comments overheard in a workplace near you:
"If I wasn't so busy I could do so much."
"It's flat out here right now, we don't know if we're coming or going."
"It's crazy, everyone is chasing their tails."
"I don't have time for that right now, I've got too much on."

There are any number of silly things people will say about their work environment - the very environment they are in charge of, or at least a part of. Why do so many talented people subject the rest of us to these cries of self-incompetence? They don't see it this way, but in reality they are screaming, "I can't manage myself out of a paper bag."

I have been observing, coaching, listening, and generally mixing with plenty of people, managers, and leaders for quite some time now. I think I have a good grasp of how *too busy* occurs. I have also been experimenting with some serial offenders over the last 13 years and I am now convinced I can explain why perfectly competent people lose their way. I'm going to share my observations and suggest some solutions.

Of course, like most 'self-improvement' situations, the offender has to first admit they are a sinner before they can get some practical advice on what they can try today, tomorrow and every day after that. After all, it's what we do and say every day that makes us fat/thin, pleasant/grumpy, interesting/boring etc.

Most of what happens in organisations is predicated on what happened in the past, i.e. everyone is influenced and shaped by what went before. People underestimate this effect. You cannot have a new future until you do something differently today. If every day is a re-run of all the past days, it is called 'getting stuck in a rut'. If you want to create something different it has to be different. If it doesn't feel different, it probably isn't different. It should feel uncomfortable for a while until your new, improved behaviours become fluent.

Most workplaces don't set out to be disorganised places. Humans have the ability to turn almost any organisation into something great or something terrible; it's what they do every day that results in the one thing or the other. Most organisations, however, do not deliberately set out to define how the workplace culture will work. Even the ones with lots of 'be good people, do good things' corporate values do not actually work out how that dream will be realised. Some do, most don't.

Deliberately setting out to achieve a positive, efficient and happy environment is a good strategy. Doing this successfully on intuition alone and without any knowledge of behavioural science is very difficult. Having a good idea of how people interact will help you understand how to get what you want. Just letting nature take its course will probably result in a garden full of weeds.

Throughout this book I refer to leaders, managers, employees, good guys, bad guys. We all fit all these descriptions from time to time. Even if you don't see yourself as a leader right now, you are going to be the leader of someone at some point.

If you've read any of my books before you will recognize the next chapter, the 'behavioural terms used in this book'. Multiple readings of this will increase your fluency when it comes to recognising what's happening around you. Your understanding of this information is proportional to the rate of your engagement in learning it.

"Perspective is worth 80 IQ points."
Alan Kay

---

2. Behavioural science terms used in this booklet

Behavioural science is the science of human behaviour; it is founded on using data and analysis to come to conclusions about what is happening in the interactions of people. Objectivity is at the core of behavioural science. Behavioural Management Techniques (BMT) is a blend of behavioural science tools and project management skills.

I have written a booklet called 'Notes on Behavioural Management Techniques' which discusses behavioural terms and offers more explanation than is covered here. This chapter should be enough to help you with the terms I mention in this booklet.

Psychologists seek to understand what is going on inside the mind, to modify these internal phenomena and in doing so achieve behaviour change. Behavioural Scientists observe the behaviour, seek to modify the external environment - which is the only thing we really have influence over anyway - and in doing so, achieve behaviour change. Behavioural science sees each person as an individual who desires a totally unique set of reinforcers from their environment (their world).

Both mainstream psychology and behavioural science are used in seeking to change behaviour. Critically, behavioural science has a greater verifiable record of achieving this and is also far easier for people to learn and apply.

A number of scientific terms are used in this booklet. These are described here:

Antecedents

An antecedent is a request or prompt; something which is attempting to drive a particular behaviour. A sign that says 'don't smoke', a speed sign, and a plan detailing how you will deliver a project are all antecedents. Antecedents are quite poor at driving behaviour if they are not paired with consequences. We are all regularly bombarded with antecedents.

Some antecedents are very good at demanding our attention. I care about the weather forecast the day before I'm going on a long walk. I care about the flight information board when I'm flying somewhere. I check what day I have to put the bins out. I look at the fuel gauge in my car when driving. Unfortunately, many work-based antecedents do not have the desired effect. Procedures, safety rules, notice boards, minutes of meetings and requests by email will all work in part, but will only work well if paired with consequences.

Behaviour

Behaviours are 'what we say and do'. They are entirely objective and measurable. It is common to see lists of behaviours in organisations that include 'communicating' or 'trust'. These are not true behaviours, as they are subjective. In contrast, 'saying "hello" to the receptionist' is a behaviour. Behaviours should fulfil the pinpointing rules (see page 6).

Consequences

The impact of consequences is the primary influencer of our behaviour. What happens to us following our behaviour will affect the likelihood of us performing the same behaviour again under similar circumstances.

Behavioural science states that there are two main consequence types that result in a behaviour occurring/recurring or stopping. They are defined as Reinforcement and Punishment. These fundamental principles are as follows:

1. If behaviour is maintained or increases it has been subject to reinforcement (R+ and R-).
2. If behaviour reduces or stops it has been subjected to punishment (P+ and P-).

The consequence in each individual case is defined by its impact on behaviour. The four consequences are summarised below. More detail can be found in the Hollin booklet *Notes on Behavioural Management Techniques.*

R+ or Positive Reinforcement: I got something I liked following my behaviour (e.g. I feel pleasure).
R- or Negative Reinforcement: I avoided something I didn't want by carrying out the behaviour (e.g. I feel relief).
P+ or Punishment: I received something I didn't want following the behaviour (e.g. I feel pain).
P- or Penalty: I had something I wanted to keep taken off me following the behaviour (e.g. I feel denied).

Extinction
Extinction is the process of being ignored. It can be very painful if you are the recipient of it. It is also a useful tool to use if you wish someone's irritating behaviour to go away. A subset of extinction is the extinction burst, an emotional outburst of some kind (usually verbal). This usually occurs when the behaviour is receding, and is a good indicator that it is.

Environment
The environment is the immediate location of a person, be it in their office, living room, their car; wherever the behaviour is occurring. A person's behaviour is mostly driven by the consequences that have followed the behaviour (or similar behaviours) in the past. The environment will dictate the consequences you experience and this includes the other people in the room, office etc. Small changes in environment can result in significant changes in the behaviour of an individual. The environment affects us and we affect the environment.

For example, imagine an office full of people. Take one person out of the office and replace them with a different person and the environment has changed. The change could be very significant depending on who left and who came in.

Pinpointing

Pinpointing is the process used to make sure that a behaviour is described accurately. Something is pinpointed when it complies with the following rules:

1. It can be seen or heard.
2. It can be measured or counted.
3. Two people would always agree that the same behaviour occurred or not.
4. It is active (something is occurring).

People who learn pinpointing can quickly develop skills which reduce the amount of assumption in their environment. This reduction of (sometimes destructive) assumptions increases the amount of informed comment, decision and discussion.

It is advisable to gather data on situations via observations and keep notes of who actually said/did what. This significantly reduces the chance of unnecessary conflict created by assumption.

Pinpointing is a very useful skill for business. Next time someone relates something to you, if you are unsure of the message you can say, "Can you pinpoint that for me please?"

Shaping

Shaping is a simple concept which is very difficult to master. It recognises that you can't get from step one to step ten in one vertical stride. You sometimes have to first write out steps two through nine and then carry them all out, one step at a time.

People sometimes tell me, "I want to say this to my boss." Before you say anything you need to predict the chances of it being received the right way by your boss. "Not very good," will often be the reply. Unfortunately, you have to shape to the goal you want to achieve, and this usually means a time-consuming set of steps which will shape the environment so that you can eventually say what you want to say and it will have the desired effect.

Shaping is not for the impatient, and a realisation that patience is the key can take time for some people. Sometimes, there is no other choice. You can't force the situation to move any faster so your options are slow shaping or nothing. Many very reinforcing tools we use these days do not help us forge a patient approach, e.g. email and voicemail. It is not naturally reinforcing taking the extra time to consider, "Is this the right thing to say? Does something else have to be achieved before I can say this and get what I want?"

Shaping is inherent in everything we learn. If you want to play an instrument, you repeat and adapt until you can play the tune. Anything that requires mastery requires repetition, reflection and adaptation. Putting a group of employees to work effectively and safely requires a leader to choose carefully who will work with whom. It requires trial and error to find the best combinations. Iteration is trying things out and seeing what the result is, adjusting and trying again – this is shaping, it works, it's the only thing that does work when building a team. This is how you succeed at getting all the right people on the bus, sat in the right seats.

> *"If you haven't felt moved by behavioural science, you haven't learned it."*
> Dr Nicole Gravina

3. *Too busy?* What are we talking about here?

People who are paid to use their brains are judged on what they produce over time. It's difficult to observe whether anyone is using their brain for the right things or not. Life would be much easier if we all had a coloured dial on the side of our head which showed if we are using our brains for the right things, but unfortunately we don't.

With help from Stephen King I have developed a working plan where I know I will always be in the mood to do at least one of three activities. These are:

1. Creating new copy
2. Editing previously written copy
3. Researching and amassing rough notes

I say to myself, "What am I in the mood for today?" Whatever the answer is, I do that. It's working fine for me; at least, I am having fun and it's producing workable copy. I ask my friends and colleagues for feedback and eventually some of my musings turn into a book.

I am in the fortunate position of being able to arrange my time in whatever way I please. Most people do not have this opportunity. Most people have their time governed by company systems and by other people. Even the very high-ups in organisations are not normally in control of how they spend their time. Someone who is caught up in a fast running stream of multiple behaviours, perhaps working in an organisation with other people, is less likely to create the opportunity to step out of the stream to view, in a calm and considered way, what's actually happening.

I spoke to someone this morning who said his new boss was insisting they discuss every detail in the business in their monthly meetings and - no surprise - the meetings last between 6 and 9 hours! I asked if he could say to his boss, "I will be here for the first 2 hours and then I'm heading off to do other stuff." Of course he said he could not say that; we can all understand why.

Someone else (a CEO) last week said he liked the idea of sorting out their many dysfunctional meetings. He wanted to know 'how' his directors would fix them. I suggested all he had to do was ask them to fix meetings, then periodically ask them how things are going. He was very uncomfortable with the idea of not knowing 'how' the meetings were going to be fixed; he was unwilling to even try delegating the task to his directors and monitoring the improvement by enquiry.

If you do it right, being a boss is not a 'busy' occupation, in fact it's the exact opposite. The successful leaders understand that they need time and space to think, and an environment where they can do the right kind of thinking.

Working long hours is not really a good indicator of whether there is a problem. I imagine lots of very happy and successful people work long hours; it's what they are doing that counts, not the number of hours that they 'work'. Some people in the *too busy* trap may well be working long hours and others exhibiting *too busy* could be working shorter hours.

Organisational rules and processes probably play a part in creating *too busy*. Organisations commonly create rules in isolation of each other. This results in a multiplicity of non-aligned rules, most of which create processes, procedures and paperwork. Some of these work well, and others do not. Business law is quite complex and voluminous, but many organisations manage governance very well. Organisational leaders work hard to satisfy the mandatory laws; it's the discretionary rules and processes that appear to get less attention.

Thirteen years of Hollin research clearly tells us that it's not the physical part of the environment or the work processes that makes businesses successful or not. It's largely the interaction between human beings that results in bad, good or great results. How leaders design the workplace environment dictates the daily behaviours. These in turn deliver the results. The environment needs to be aligned so that the workers' daily behaviours lead automatically to the desired results. The key is what people do and say, every day. A great leader I had the pleasure of working with, Alasdair Cathcart, said, "When it comes to production, environment will beat process every day of the week." Therefore leaders - not processes - are responsible for making themselves and their people either productive or *too busy*.

The removal of barriers to success is a key leadership tenet. Random, perhaps out-of-control consequences in the workplace environment need to be fielded with aplomb by a competent leader. Fielded and deftly removed from the environment so the future can be better. For the last thirteen years I have been asking people the question, "What is the percentage of stupid stuff you do at work every day that you wouldn't do if you had a choice?" The answers are varied but I'm often told that it's more than 50%. More than 50% stupid stuff in any day, and these organisations still exist? Well, survive, not thrive, but it does highlight the opportunity that they could do much better.

> *"A man is never more truthful than when he acknowledges himself a liar."*
>
> Mark Twain

4. What does too busy look like?

In an organisational hierarchy *too busy* is hard to detect from above; it's easier to observe it from below. Someone said to me, "We have no time for the softer sides of leadership, we are all *too busy*" and I responded, "If you could stop focusing your attention upwards in your organisation then you could use that time for leading the people below you." *Too busy*, to most workers, looks like disorganised, careless and insecure.

Recently, a group of directors commented to me that being *too busy* and having a jam-packed day which started early and finished late was just the way it was in their industry; a self-fulfilling rationalisation if ever there was one!

I am sure no-one sets out to look disorganised, careless or insecure but *too busy* is very common indeed. It's so common that when you observe someone who organises their time really well, they stand out as calm, approachable, and trustworthy. Take a look around. How many 'calm and approachable' people do you see? Do you trust them?

Too busy also causes very strong feelings of uncertainty for the victims lower down or outside the organisation. You can observe the person who isn't returning your calls or emails walking in and out of the building, and as you watch them your feelings of anger can increase day by day. This effect is called 'dirty pain'; suffering someone else's dysfunctional behaviour in silence while it eats away at you.

Of course they are completely unaware of your anger and frustration. You can correct this extinction experience in many ways, but the most effective method will be devising an improvement shaping plan and speaking to them face to face. Your quest right now is to change the personal consequences of your subject person from 'I can ignore this' to 'I can't ignore this'.

We are talking about two separate worlds here, the world of the *too busy* person and your world (not forgetting that you may well be *too busy* also). You are vying with others, I suppose, for the attention of the person in question; it's a competition for someone's time and attention. The *too busy* person allots seemingly random discretionary time for random people. It might appear random but it's not; it's really them aligning themselves to the reinforcers in their environment. They are responding to the most threatening (R-) or the most fun stuff (R+), and they will respond wherever the most potential reinforcement appears.

If you are a *too busy* person, then you will be doing this too - spending your time avoiding threats and seeking out moments of pleasure. That is what happens to someone when they allow their environment to dictate their behaviour rather than controlling their environment themselves. Take charge of your own environment. People who are passive about their environment usually get what they deserve; they rarely get lucky.

The victims of *too busy* are unlikely to believe that they are the problem: "I get all this stuff from my boss, and he's on my back all the time; when am I supposed to be answering the 100 emails a day that come in?" This perspective screams 'learned helplessness' - when someone has spent too long thinking, "I am a victim and I can't do anything about this." It is a very sad thing to see.

Of course, a common downstream impact of *too busy* is the bottleneck that it creates - the person who has become chronically disorganised is likely to be creating a paralysis within their teams. Imagine working for this person; they have known they needed to get the report written for the last five weeks, and with two days to go they wake up from their coma and try to pass that job on to you.

It's possible to take a side step if this person is a peer or colleague, but harder avoid if they're your boss.

One of the other by-products of *too busy* is the frustration of observing the *too busy* person wasting time on jollies, boondoggles or opulent corporate entertainment activities in the name of business development. It's a slippery slope; the corporate world is peppered with tempting opportunities for people to fall by the wayside and many people do. It takes integrity and self-discipline to avoid these traps. Engineer temptation out so you can fail fewer times than you otherwise would.

> *"Why don't you stop telling me how busy you are and just get on with your work?"*
>
> Janet Slater

5. Too busy as a protective shield

Some people who are *too busy* fill their days with avoidance behaviours. This person is avoiding doing the activities they should be doing and they are doing something else instead. The behaviours you are observing are what this person is doing and obviously you can't observe what someone isn't doing.

Avoidance is where someone is doing something else because the thing they should be doing is too hard/scary/confrontational/embarrassing/energy-sapping, whatever. In an earlier book I mentioned my occasional habit of cleaning the office when I get stuck with my writing. It's avoidance behaviour; it is not because I have an obsessive desire to have a clean office.

Too busy is used as a shield to hide behind or worn as a badge of honour by some people while they partake in more reinforcing avoidance behaviours. It's too easy for some people to respond to only selective emails, attend the easy, fun meetings or check and re-check a report for spelling errors rather than finishing and submitting it. Avoidance behaviours also make it less likely that mistakes will be made - little work is done, so there are fewer opportunities to make errors. It also makes the *too busy* person less approachable so people don't ask them to do things. It explains why office politics are so popular - to some it's more fun than work.

Moaning about colleagues and bosses at the water cooler, in the kitchen, in the canteen; it's all safe and reinforcing. In many workplaces it is socially acceptable to say, "I'm *too busy*" and it's reinforcing. In fact, to say otherwise would result in punishment from many of the other people there. It's common to hear the *too busy* people who stay late every night complain about the person who consistently leaves promptly, regardless of how productive either party is.

Using the *too busy* shield then leads to another common avoidance behaviour. A lack of confidence in one's ability to improvise under pressure will mean that these people will avoid putting themselves in even slightly unpredictable situations. This leads to people electing not to challenge dysfunctions in, for example, company processes or in other people's behaviours. The potential confrontational fallout is perceived to be more hassle that it's worth. They rationalise their silence by saying to themselves, "I'm *too busy* for this." There's a lot of people out there who are hypnotised by the perceived complexity of their job. *Too busy* syndrome provides them with the perfect escape route.

On one of our past courses a Project Director went online and viewed every homework assignment on his course but didn't complete any them. He didn't attend any further modules after module one. Nor did he say "I am not doing this course". A unique *too busy* excuse was used for each of the six non-attended modules. Also, none of his people said anything to him about this. When I tried to see him, he was *too busy*, and his PA was very apologetic.

He attempted to control everything in his field of vision with minute attention to detail and no attention to the overall goal. His avoidance behaviours generalised into other areas: he avoided anything which would put him in a place where he had to rely upon his own ability to persuade or charm or at a very basic level - lead.

This Project Director hid behind the contract for the project. This type of behaviour is quite common and can be observed in many situations. People hide behind the law and its various forms; safety law, finance law, quality assurance procedures, governance rules.

It's the last refuge of the leader who simply can't lead, the manager who can't manage, and the parent who, for whatever reason, can't nurture.

Working for this kind of leader inevitably means that all project reports will have to be re-written multiple times. People will be asked to appear at meetings loaded down with all the conceivable information the leader may require. Meetings will last many hours, consuming everyone's time. Minutes of meetings will be voluminous. Many more people will join the ranks of the *too busy* and are handed their *too busy* shield as they walk in the door each and every day.

There was a time when this scenario would have irritated me; I now believe that these situations are good observational fodder and useful content for our courses as we demonstrate to our clients' course attendees that other people have problem managers too. This dysfunctional leader was behaving out loud in plain sight, and he's not the only one.

> *"Politicians like to panic, they need activity. It is their substitute for achievement."*
> Sir Humphrey Appleby, Yes Minister

6. How realistic are we at knowing what we spend our time on?

Some people are great at managing and prioritising their time and some are not. The ones that are good at recording where they spend their time are also good at keeping tabs on what they actually do: How much they manage to focus on value-adding activities e.g. coaching and creative pursuits. The hopeless time-keepers are also hopeless at measuring what they do. It's one thing for them to say they want to improve; it's another to actually shoot themselves in the foot and offer up the proof that they can't manage their activities or their time properly.

Observing others and how they spend their time is a very interesting pursuit indeed. Humans will go wherever the maximum reinforcement can be found; not the delayed reinforcement, but the instant stuff. You can see people chasing reinforcers if you look hard enough, you can easily learn how to observe their little idiosyncrasies. I would say that many people, lots of the time, aren't doing what they say they want to do, day to day. They do whatever their environment dictates they will do. People are either the victims or the masters of their own environment.

Few people step outside this basic rule of behaviour. Even the experts in behavioural science cannot escape that they are subject to whatever environment they find themselves in. Getting a hold of our own behaviour is very difficult, especially for employees who are working in an environment dominated by someone else. That is because we can't change our behaviour easily. In fact, it is the wrong thing to try. This direct approach doesn't work. The successful but indirect route is to change the environment. All behaviours will always align with the environment. Pretending that other people cannot impact our behaviour is silly.

I gave a presentation a while ago and argued that humans are like dolphins. Where dolphins endlessly pursue large quantities of fish, humans pursue reinforcers. Humans will go wherever their history of experiences tells them the reinforcers are. I like what I know and I know what I like, I liked it last time, I will like it/him/her again next time. Of course the same applies for the things I didn't like; over time I will get very good at avoiding the things I don't like. Actually most people are expert in avoiding the things or the people they don't like.

So in summary, the good guys don't need to record what they intend to do in a week because they can already manage their time effectively. These are the people who make it look effortless. That is because they aren't expending any effort trying to resist their environment or use self-discipline. They have done the pre-work to create the conditions for future success; their environment works for them.

The bad guys, who do need to record their plans and see how good they are with their time, will never record it. Another paradox; the really bad guys need the most help but don't want it. Again, the good news is that each person working in the environment of the really bad guys can influence their behaviour. If the bad guy won't measure him/herself, then perhaps you and your cadre of like-minded people should collect data on them, or more subtly, collect data on everyone (including them).

What can we do to show people what they are actually spending their time on? It could be worthwhile creating a work group 'project', especially if a group of people agree they want to achieve a gradual adjustment of their environment. Incremental change is hard to detect and manage. This group could measure some current activities with a view to creating simple shaping steps towards the goal of a more reinforcing workplace for everyone. One simple and easy change per week will add up to a considerable amount in a year.

The graphic below compares activity with the value it creates. Asking people to populate these boxes is an interesting exercise. If they are being candid then the most populated box is likely to be 'High Activity', 'Low Value'. The least populated box will probably be 'High Value', 'Low Activity' – this one, of course, is where the money is!

Too Busy Trap

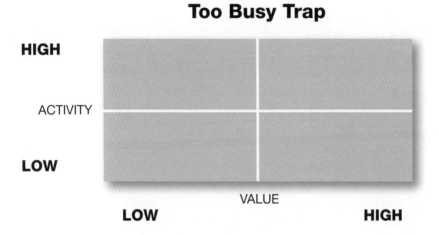

Activity - How much time do you spend on these tasks?
Value - How significant are these tasks in achieving business targets?

6.1 What else could I do? Something simple that doesn't take up too much time!

Rating scales are good, they take no time to do, and you rate yourself so there's no threat involved. It will help you find out just how much of a sinner you are! Consider using a simple scoring system on your schedule/diary:

1. An upward arrow for time spent with bosses/clients.
2. A sideways arrow for time spent with peers.
3. A downward arrow for time spent with subordinates.

This will be a good indicator of whether the balance of your time is aligned to your desires and the needs of your people and the organisation. If you want to move to another level with this scoring process, you can make a mark that indicates if the time you spent was also valuable. It's still true that the primary function of any great leader is to create some more great leaders for the organisation and this can't be achieved by permanently hob-knobbing with peers and bosses.

Of course, you cannot beat writing down what you will do every week on a Monday morning then going through it on Friday afternoon and marking it up with what you actually did. This is another one of those ideas always taken up by the people who don't need it and never taken up by the people that do need it!

Some people over-simplistically look at 'courage' as the major component in changing people's behaviour. I think 'knowledge of what is actually happening' is a more useful vehicle to assist the process of behavioural change. This is also because 'courage' is difficult to measure and it changes day by day. Sure, you can list what you definitely will and won't do and fill the space between with many graduated shaping steps. Quite a few people have done this successfully, but again it's only usually the enthusiasts who will make the time to do this. The attractive thing about using knowledge of what is actually happening as the primary change agent is that it's easy to observe and measure; we are talking about your environment and your effect on other people's behaviour here.

If you give someone else feedback on something they did, they cannot un-hear it. They can pretend to ignore it but that's not the same thing. It's the same effect for a team of people conspiring to deliver some new consequences for the behaviour of a bully. There is very little the bully can do about others adjusting the environment they share with them. This is especially true if the bully only detects that something has changed but cannot pinpoint what it actually is and how it happened.

While potentially awkward, this approach generates a different and uncertain environment. Doing so creates a vacuum for someone to fill with new and better consequences for all. As more people can be persuaded to gradually adjust how they respond to others, then more and more workplace environments will be improved for the better.

If the intended recipient of changes in the environment does not realise the full content of the feedback but can still detect a change in the environment, then the feedback must have been delivered effectively. The goal is to effect a subtle change in the environment. If you all decided to glance out of the window when the office bully says a trigger word, and you all glance out of the window, the bully will notice something is different, and that's the goal: Create a vacuum you can now fill with something you want. Lots of people are uncomfortable with 'environment changing games'. However, they can be very effective when carried out well and they can be very funny; what's the worst thing that can happen?

> *"The trickster's function is to break taboos, create mischief, stir things up. In the end the trickster gives people what they really want, some sort of freedom."*
>
> Tim Robbins

7. How do some people fill their days?

I am a lucky guesser. Here is a list of things people get up to in order to fill their days with reinforcers as opposed to filling their days doing the right things both for them and their organisation.

1. Getting caught in lots of non-value adding ping-pong emails.
2. Fighting off threats created by office politics.
3. Attending meetings the boss is attending.
4. Attending boring meetings.
5. Joining in all the events that the senior people attend.
6. Working on bonusable objectives near to the closing date.
7. Nagging people on email for missing information/reports.
8. Walking around to talk to the people they like.
9. Looking at progress spreadsheets too often.
10. Attending all corporate road shows.
11. Whining about the changes to the company car scheme whilst maximising their mileage claims.
12. Complaining with ill-disguised self-importance about how they are *too busy*.

This person has too little reinforcement available for their work and likely no sense of urgency in their environment either. The leader responsible for this situation has failed to create the right environment. The chances of this person saying, "I am *too busy*" is very high.

This list of daily avoidance activity was supplied to us by a disgruntled employee who really didn't like their boss:

1. Watching and passing on the funny stuff I get sent on the web.
2. Answering the irritating emails, copying them to everyone.
3. Getting involved in irrelevant pissing contests on email.
4. Checking out the job scene.
5. Going to the fun meetings and having fun.
6. Working out reasons why something can't be done and then applying them.
7. Getting imaginative with timesheets and expenses.
8. Moaning about other people with my colleagues.
9. Maximising my LinkedIn followers.
10. Finding a reason to go on a good trip somewhere.
11. Going out of the office for coffee.

Of course this isn't a *too busy* list; it's the list of activities of someone seeking out reinforcers because there aren't many in the workplace. The chances of this person often saying, "I am *too busy*" is also very high. Of course, they could do something about their predicament but they have decided not to, for whatever reason.

What's interesting about both of these lists is that the behaviour is contingent on the current environment and the environment will have to change for any new behaviour to emerge. It's not as hard as losing weight or giving up bad habits; it's much harder than that, as there are multiple relationships to align to achieve a change. These environments were created by people and over time dysfunction has been generated and reinforced. Testing workplace environments regularly and correcting them with feedback is the way to avoid this kind of organisational dysfunction.

A dieting analogy is useful here; it's much easier to give up smoking or drinking too much alcohol than it is to temper eating habits. Why? You don't have to smoke or drink alcohol to live, but you still have to eat, so the temptation to overeat is ever-present. Moderating a behaviour is harder than stopping it altogether.

If you want to change the way other people treat you, then you have to adjust your environment. Giving up a behaviour is easier than adjusting a behaviour, especially if all the temptations that led to the behaviour in the first place are currently evident in your environment. Changing the environment is going to take some planning and some careful application, so just a little awareness and self-discipline is required. Removing all wine from the house will affect the likelihood of it being drunk. Not buying any cream cakes will stave off temptation. We need a payoff in order to successfully adjust our behaviour, and this leads us to the motivational traps.

> *"One man alone can be pretty dumb sometimes, but for real bona fide stupidity, there ain't nothing can beat teamwork."*
>
> Edward Abbey

8. Motivational traps

This chapter was originally produced by Allison Reynolds from Ryan Olson's material; many thanks to both of you.

Why do so many people fall into the trap of making themselves *too busy*? Nature has a part to play in this. Humans have evolved primarily for survival and this has created a flaw in our design. At least, it's a flaw for those who no longer need to fight for security, warmth and food.

In order to be able to survive, to eat and to avoid getting eaten long enough to reproduce, humans have finely tuned their activities to maximise the reinforcers in their immediate environment. They have also minimised the amount of effort it takes to do so. After all, we wouldn't survive for very long if we used up more energy finding food and keeping clear of predators than we were actually able to consume. This legacy has led to some common motivational traps which lure us into bad habits. These traps are called:

1. **The payoff trap**
2. **The effort trap**
3. **The rare event trap**
4. **The sneaky trap**

8.1 The payoff trap

Nature has shaped humans to maximise the numbers of daily reinforcers they receive. We are therefore very susceptible to behaviours that get us an immediate payoff. We will engage in behaviours that are comfortable, convenient or pleasurable, even though they may not be in our long term interest. Of course this means we will avoid behaviours that do not satisfy this basic need, even if they are important to us.

Some basic payoff trap activities for people could be: Eating unhealthy food, drinking alcohol, smoking cigarettes, gambling etc. All these activities have a pretty instant payoff. Most people these days have mortgages, loans or credit cards; these products allow people to have what they want now and pay for it later. Their immediate needs are satisfied right now, just like nature intended.

When it comes to the workplace there are just as many distractions to suck people into behaviours that get them reinforcement now even though they might have long term downsides: Sending emails rather than waiting to speak to someone face to face; attending pointless meetings to keep the boss happy; doing everyone else's job for them instead of figuring out how to delegate, because the result happens quicker.

Studies have shown that people are so sensitive to the immediacy of reinforcement they will often opt for less today rather than wait until tomorrow for more. I guess this is why so many people fall into the trap of reacting to their environment rather than mastering it. The former delivers lots of reinforcement today, the latter delivers much more, but at some point down the line. The delayed reinforcement effect is the reason giving up smoking, drinking alcohol, or over-eating are so hard. Of course, this is also why breaking out of the *too busy* trap is so hard.

8.2 The effort trap

If the payoff trap is the quickest path to reinforcement then the effort trap is the path of least resistance; how to get what you want with the least amount of effort. For example, ordering a takeaway rather than cooking a meal; watching television rather than having a conversation; playing sports on a games console rather than going for a walk. It's easy to see how people turn into couch potatoes.

Organisations are awash with people who have fallen for the effort trap: sending emails to avoid the hassle of speaking to someone on the phone or face to face; checking minute levels of detail on a spreadsheet when they should be figuring out how to stop the programme slipping any further; accepting the status quo even though they are desperately unhappy with it - it's all just less effort. Reinforcement abounds as people feel they achieved their task right away and get to tick it off their list.

To compound the problem, many behaviours are subject to both the payoff trap and the effort trap. Junk food tastes better and takes less effort to prepare, sending email is quicker and you avoid the hassle of dealing with people... We don't stand much chance really.

8.3 The rare event trap

Some punishing consequences of behaviour don't tend to happen very often, making us susceptible to the rare event trap. If people don't perceive a downside for a particular behaviour then there will be no reinforcement for doing the alternative. Take speeding down the motorway for example; people drive faster than 70mph because they really don't think anything bad is going to happen to them. The brain finds it so difficult to imagine that anything bad will happen, when the last 50/100/1000 times we sped, nothing bad happened and nothing bad happened to the people close to us.

Many people work in an environment with a distinct lack of feedback. A lack of frequent and accurate constructive feedback can trick people into thinking that their behaviour is OK, because nothing bad has happened so far. The chances are that the first time they know there is a problem, their performance is so far off-plan it's too late to recover. Safety suffers badly from the rare event trap, especially in the 'civilised world' where bad injuries and fatalities are rare events.

Many investigations of injuries and incidents have shown that it wasn't the first time the unsafe behaviour had occurred, but it was the first time the unsafe behaviour resulted in an injury. Previous repetitions of the unsafe behaviour had not resulted in pain or threat, and therefore, over time, it became a false 'safe act'.

This leads us on to the fourth and final trap, the sneaky trap.

8.4 The sneaky trap

Perhaps the deadliest of all the traps is the sneaky trap. You may have heard the grizzly tale of boiling a frog. If you drop a frog into a pan of boiling water, it'll jump straight back out, but put the frog in cold water and turn the temperature up slowly and it'll stay right there and die.

This is the sneaky trap. The undesirable consequences of the behaviour are so slow to accumulate that by the time people realise they have a problem it's often too late to easily reverse the damage. If a person consumes just an extra 500 calories a week, ten years down the line their weight will have gradually crept up significantly. If people spend all of their free time using a computer, smart phone etc, then their personal relationships will gradually decline. I sit in cafes and restaurants and observe couples, families, all heads down into their hand-held device. Who said the art of conversation was dying? Of course I approve of people, heads down, reading this book wherever they are!

People can become victims of their workplace environment if they just keep turning up to all those meetings, and feeding the endless beast of email. Are they *too busy* to take even a day to step back and figure out how to do something different? It's possible that they may be lucky one day and get fired. If not, there is the prospect of waking up 30 years down the road and realising they have become just another bureaucrat. Now the fate of the frog doesn't sound so bad.

The point is that as human beings we are all susceptible to motivational traps. Unfortunately, many leadership behaviours have a delayed payoff and take more effort. I guess this is why so many fall in to the *too busy* trap. However, all is not lost. If we recognise that our current environment is getting us multiple *too busy* behaviours then all that is required is to actively take a hold of that environment and build in more immediate reinforcement for doing the things that add the most long term value. It's all just about tipping the odds back in your favour. Great leaders, and we are all leaders of someone, aren't blessed with superior willpower; they're just very good at managing their own environment to get more of what they want from themselves.

Beware of the motivational traps - adjust your environment to stave off '*too busy*'.

> *"The secret of life is enjoying the passage of time."*
> James Taylor

9. How much damage can one *too busy* person do?

Oh, plenty is the short answer. Behaviour is contingent on the environment, and the environment changes every time a new person walks in or an incumbent walks out. The environment changes every time someone gets a promotion. Let's face it, the environment changes a lot over time. There are many personalities out there, so many that we can't count them, least of all stereotype them. I have witnessed some individuals do incredibly inspirational things. I have seen other people cause misery, ruining other people's work lives, even still influencing their victim's behaviour after they are long gone.

One person can affect the whole workplace culture. I often ask people if there is a notable good or bad person in their organisation. I will get a guarded response initially but in no time at all the names fly about in conversations over coffee and sometimes in group discussions.

We're not taught at school how to identify the good guys but we do learn quickly who the bad guys are; our survival instincts kick in at an early age. One way of spotting the bad guys is that they are more likely to focus on 'effect' (*too busy*) rather than integrity (calm). It follows that the good guys will do the opposite. I have also observed that the exceptional leaders display self-control, and focus entirely on the person talking to them. They focus on how their reaction is perceived ahead of the subject matter itself, and this is a sign of great emerging leadership.

You already know who you would take with you, and you know who you wouldn't take with you if you left your current job and started up your own company. Both of these imagined scenarios are usually true. Both these scenarios can be pinpointed. Just take 15 seconds to think about who those people in your workplace might be. All the individuals you are thinking about exhibit behaviours that can be pinpointed. This is the easy part of using behavioural science, all you are doing is observing and writing stuff down. You haven't challenged anyone to a duel yet.

Here is an example of a destructive manager, whose behaviour created considerable amounts of *too busy* among those affected by him:

This manager was the consummate bureaucrat, a massively inflated ego with implausible levels of self-importance considering he was just a bloke working for a utility company. However, over time, he managed to set up a culture of fear and loathing which affected almost everyone in the organisation and within its suppliers and contractors. "What can we do about Geoffrey," people used to say. "He's making our lives impossible. We spend all our time either responding to his threatening letters or complaining about him, we are not actually getting any work done. Everyone is *too busy* chasing their tail." This is a common story - people 'chasing sticks' and taking them back to the boss.

What Geoffrey was doing was having his own intellectual pissing contest. He would write many letters on points of minutiae from within the contract, he would pick at any sore, he would zoom in on items the suppliers had not adhered to - mostly in terms of deliverables for reports, certificates, any minor contractual requirement. The whole picture was laced with irritating bureaucratic deliverables, all originally put into the contract by Geoffrey.

Geoffrey had a lot of energy, a lot of time to spend at work and was clearly not interested in the big picture. Geoffrey's aggression was usually delivered in a passive aggressive way. This case is a great example of one person dragging everyone else down to his level of mistrust and eagerness to catch folks out, consuming everyone else's time in the process; everybody was *too busy*, seven days a week *too busy*.

I made a number of suggestions for the others around him to make changes in his environment but the team were unwilling to try anything out, such were the levels of fear created by this man. The *too busy* effect on the team was the very thing that stopped them solving the dysfunctional situation Geoffrey had created and the situation that they were inadvertently reinforcing.

How do some *too busy* people create the spectacular levels of fear and loathing that exists? I suspect it starts small and then quickly opens out wider as the perpetrator of the destructive behaviours receives nothing but reinforcement for their antics. Of the people who have been labelled destructive managers there are some constants:

1. They will have the ability to turn on the charm.
2. They commonly have an obsessive attachment to a qualification or membership of something that smells exclusive.
3. Their ego will always be close to the surface.
4. They will fundamentally believe that they are working for the good of all.
5. They will demonstrate a penchant for one-upmanship.
6. There will be "I believe" statements sprinkled around.
7. They will rationalise their impatience with people as caring about the business. "Why do I get mad? I get mad because I care so much about this business."
8. Communication will be random and unpredictable.
9. They will not understand the downstream impact of their behaviour (although they say they do).
10. They will claim they can take feedback - danger, it's not true.
11. They will play favourites with staff, suppliers, and peers in their industry group.
12. They are unlikely to read a book like this.

Being truly open to honest feedback requires massive self-control in what is said in response to the feedback. It's the kind of mammoth self-control most of us don't exhibit very often. Responding well to all feedback is very hard to do.

Recently one of our 'senior team' courses reached module three, at which point the Managing Director could not attend. The deputy MD was there and he exhibited a number of new behaviours in front of the rest of the remaining eleven people on the team. Feet on the table, speaking up much more, voicing many more opinions than he had done during modules one and two, nipping out to take 'urgent calls'. A number of clear power plays were performed and of course observed by the professional behavioural trainer in the room.

The trainer resisted the temptation to ask him if he'd read any books on body language. This is the kind of easily observable change in behavioural norms when the environment shifts. If anyone else in the room had been looking, they too would have observed what the trainer saw (most of the others in the room were also permanently set to *too busy* and therefore distracted and didn't see what was there in plain sight).

Most folks don't look out for power plays. There is a lot of fun to be had by observing alpha males in full display of their feathers (not forgetting all that screeching they do).

9.1 Damage caused by leaders who focus on loss aversion

This *too busy* person will do whatever is easy. If the choice is wealth creation or loss aversion they will always pick loss aversion, because it's easy and also because humans are hard-wired to do just that. It's the same choice as focusing on antecedents or consequences; there's no competition because it's much easier to write antecedents than devise effective consequences.

When they have something important they need to say to everyone in the organisation, loss-aversion-focused leaders write a letter to 'all staff', send it by email and copy to everyone. It's easy and fast. If they took a second to think of the consequences of the letter or email they may well reconsider, but they don't have a second to spare to reflect. One of the great paradoxes highlighted by the folks that are *too busy* is their tendency to micromanage a lot. It appears to stem from a combination of a lack of trust in others and the need to feel as if they are making things happen. Leadership expert Marshall Goldsmith calls this 'adding too much value'.

Micromanagement is an aspect of loss aversion and has more to do with a failure to create a successful workplace environment than anything else. This means there is little time for thinking; for the protagonist, micromanaging is reinforcing, it's exciting, in the same way that careering down a mountain on skis or a bicycle is exciting. These adrenaline junkie leaders can be observed; can you think of someone like this? What do they spend their time on? Can you write that down and analyse it? I guarantee that there will be clues for finding the escape route within your analysis.

Micromanagers are the ones who look over the shoulders of their direct reports and try to talk to everyone in the organisation. Anyone can busy themselves rejecting expenses, questioning a trip, questioning expenditure on courses, training, safety equipment; it's easy!
In fact, there are well known behavioural mechanisms at work here; these tasks are reinforcing. This micromanager genuinely feels like they achieved something and made a difference.

9.2 The too busy yet befuddled, well-meaning boss

This is the gentle sort who is nice to people, too nice maybe; a bit sycophantic, a survivor, a middle manager. You can imagine a life completely overwhelmed with *too busy* avoidance behaviours. They sound earnest in meetings, turn up on time, look respectable, are polite, don't rise to goading, don't upset any of the bosses, will deliver tough-sounding feedback to peers and others but always within safe limits.

These people are really frustrating. They are not mean, they will not blame their boss for everything bad, they will talk to you and help you but somehow you walk away feeling like you are being held at arm's length. They are not dishonest to you, they have values, and they will honour their agreements with you. You always get the feeling they want the conversation to end soon. You do not have the warm feeling that this person is going to save your skin when it comes down to a fight. It's what these people don't do that causes the stress.

Great leaders understand that it's their job to create an environment for people to be able to succeed. True leaders create a place where people can achieve their best, where people can thrive, where you get a contagious enthusiasm, where the business is soaked in discretion, and is the kind of business that makes good profits over a sustained period of time. The befuddled nice person is not going to make the key leadership contribution for the organisation. If the company is successful then that means someone else is doing the leading.

One of the primary functions of leaders is to develop a good relationship with their people. Without a relationship of some kind it's impossible to have a meaningful dialogue. Part of developing that key relationship is demonstrating caring, including training needs. Business leader Alasdair Cathcart urges other leaders in his organisation to focus on succession. He asks, "Who are the two or three people in your team that could be your successor? What are their needs? If you were to move on tomorrow, imagine each person on your list sat in your chair, doing your job. What skills are they in need of?" This is an excellent way of focusing on genuine development needs.

Also some successful companies delegate the choice of training to each individual. They will offer training courses but the decision as to 'what course and when' is ultimately made by each individual and always supported by their leader. People like having the last word on their own development needs, it's empowering.

> *"A man hears what he wants to hear and disregards the rest."*
> Paul Simon

10. What can I do about these destructive characters?

There are a few stereotypical *too busy* destructive characters described in the last chapter.

The first safe step towards an acceptable solution is to start triangulating your own frame of reference and ask trusted colleagues for their opinion on what's happening in the environment. Then ask them to observe and pinpoint what the *too busy* 'bad guy' is doing. Soon you will have a stack of pinpointed observations you can analyse. You can then decide on the next steps.

The goal for any improvement is to see if you can adjust the workplace environment. The recipient for the resulting change does not have to realise you have embarked on a plan. You do not have to be the boss to achieve this, anyone can do it. Of course you will have to judge how risky some of these things would be. Peter Block has a saying: "The helpless and distressed working for tyrannical boss." There are some people who would readily identify with this description.

Of course some people have never been in this kind of predicament. If that's you then this next section might shock you, but I assure you it is a sad reality for some other people. If this content doesn't fit your particular frame of reference then you are welcome to skip to the next chapter. By reading on, you will see a sample of what some people's miserable workplace experiences are like.

10.1 Last resorts

Most people do not want to stand up to the 'too scary' person in their life for obvious and understandable reasons. The prospect of standing up to a difficult *too busy* character in a straight fight is not a solution for most people. However, here are some things that have been said to supposedly 'too scary' people in workplaces the world over:

- "Can you repeat that, it was a bit complicated."
- "It feels like you have an unusual take on the agenda for this meeting."
- "I'm sorry but are we here to (fill in the purpose of the project/business)? Just checking."
- "Of all the things you just asked for, which ones are you happy to pay extra for?" (If you can make something cost more; bullies hate it if the money trail ends with them.)
- "I'm sorry but I'm finding your constant untrusting comments rather tiring now."
- "We are trying to run a business here. In order to achieve that I will need the co-operation of the staff. I can achieve that but right now you are just pissing everyone off. What about you talk to me and I'll translate what you want to them."
- "I'm afraid you have created a bit of a comic caricature for yourself, I am trying to control it but you're going to have to help me out here."
- "I have been in business for many years and I have never seen good come out of your style of management, only upsets and overspends. Would you like me to give you any more feedback?"
- "This is becoming tiresome. How about you just write down your gripes and I'll take them away and sort them out for you?"
- "It seems you don't care about pissing people off."
- "Can I let everyone else go back to work and you can just rant at me? It will be better for the business."
- "This could still be a great business. To be honest it's your call; this could also easily continue to go pear-shaped, it's really up to you."
- "I hate to see someone make a fool of themselves, but in your case I'm willing to make an exception."

Some of these phrases are more robust than others, but there is always a choice of what to say. Prepare your own version of some statements like these in advance. Memorise and practise out loud the ones you are prepared to say to the scary person.

I have coached numerous people in the 'helpless and distressed' category. I always argue that every dysfunctional situation can be turned from unpleasant to tolerant and even pleasant. Here are some ideas to help you improve your enjoyment in meetings:

For individuals:

- Prior to the meeting, write down what you think the other attendees will say, and what responses they are going to get and from who. Tick them off and score yourself at the end.
- Prior to the meeting make notes about who is going to push one particular agenda, score yourself on your accuracy of predicting the content of the meeting.
- Record your meetings (just buy a digital recorder and place it on the table in front of you). You can make most meetings more efficient by doing this; it stymies the verbal behaviours of the meeting blowhards.

It's better to work in groups than try to fix an unpleasant boss on your own. A team might try these ideas:

- Arrange for the people in the room look out of the window when the tyrant says a particular word (this is hilarious if everyone joins in. You need a trigger word the tyrant uses commonly).
- Everyone furiously write stuff down when he is talking, looking furtive.
- People in the room look at the floor (again if you can agree a trigger word, it's funny).
- People all stand up and leave at the agreed time rather than sitting through the overrun (this also requires a considerable amount of courage).
- Someone asks, "Let's have a show of hands, does anybody enjoy these meetings?" The rest agree to vote for 'no'.

Of course these suggestions require you to get together with other people and plan a strategy. It seems silly in the cold light of day that this amount of trouble is required to deal with one dysfunctional person, but sadly in many cases it's true. It's well worth taking the trouble to fix dysfunctions early. Tolerating unpleasant workplace cultures for years on end is a pointless thing to do, especially when they can be very easy to fix. I have observed that the people who stand up to bullies usually win in the end. Perhaps not in their current job or even current organisation but the effect of standing up for what's right has a great impact on their future tolerance of potential bullies. Great leaders stand up to bullies.

A fantastic project manager I know told me that he was once in a big meeting with his director and had tried to make a point on a number of occasions but failed each time to get the director's attention. While the meeting was still active he decided to phone the director up in the room, and of course the director picked up. Phil then said "I've been trying to get your attention for half an hour now…" and everyone else fell about laughing. Destructive characters don't usually know what to do when someone lampoons them in public.

> *"When people make themselves too busy, others are disinclined to help them."*
>
> Rachel Edwards

11. How do you get out of this *too busy* trap?

11.1 Successful leaders

The successful leaders create wealth, run successful organisations, deliver projects, and engender happy families. You will observe that they focus on the people that work directly for them, bringing out the best in them. They have the foresight to exploit opportunities and figure out how to utilise all their resources to create a successful organisation.

We all get 24 hours every day. The successful leaders get their time management right, spend the right proportion of their time with direct reports and customers and spend no time at all on micromanagement. We can all observe these qualities in great leaders with admiration. Last year I was asked what my ideal leader would look like - what behaviours they would exhibit - and I produced this list. This would be my ideal leader. In fact, it was on a number of occasions.

From my perspective, my ideal leader:
- Turns up on time for our meetings.
- Honours their obligations.
- Returns my emails and phone calls in a timely fashion.
- Stays silent while I am speaking. Switches their smartphone off when we meet or ignores incoming emails and calls when we are speaking.
- Goes out of their way for me.
- Does something thoughtful for me sporadically.
- Makes time for my personal development.
- Gives me the time and space to do my job without constant interruption.

- Tells me when I did well.
- Gives me honest and timely feedback when I don't do so well.
- Credits me when they repeat my ideas.
- Recommends me to others.
- Doesn't bullshit me, others around us, or our customers.
- Is talked about in positive terms by everyone else.
- Solicits feedback.
- Responds well to bad news.
- Encourages those around them to also behave in this way.
- Says inspirational things.
- Wins work which is deliverable and profitable.
- Encourages everyone to be truthful.
- Encourages everyone to deliver praise when they see it.
- Deals with poor performance in a timely, decisive and fair way.

This makes a handy aspirational list. Some people have it pinned above their desk to remind them of the goal.

11.2 Resisting the temptation of the too busy trap

The thing that makes the *too busy* trap alluring is that the natural consequences of the other behaviours in people's workplace environments make falling into the trap almost inevitable. Our inner radar is constantly scanning for reinforcers and punishers in our immediate environment. We are constantly making decisions that veer us away from punishers and move us toward reinforcers. This is the fundamental truth behind the science of human behaviour.

If your basic motivation is to make the world of work a better place then there is a good chance that you will notice when you are being dragged to the dark (or light) side. A meeting request from someone you don't like, one from someone you do like. An email from someone you don't like and one from someone you do like. Your decision making process is likely to allot your time to the people you like the most. People tend to shy away from some of the very things they should be addressing; we all do, for multiple and obvious reasons.

Recognising these things and planning to remove them from your environment requires booking a day out to get organised. List who you do and don't want to get emails from, list who you do and don't want calls from, manage the others out of your world of work, politely but assertively. Decide which meetings you will go to (and not) and state it. Set clear expectations to others and most people will respect your wishes. Tidying up a schedule is not that hard, creating a diary with plenty of space is easy, staying at home and clearing backlogs is not hard: this is the weeding the garden part of getting organised. Once this is done then future weeding is easy if it's done every few days.

11.3 Behavioural models - The performance equation

Dr Ryan Olson is a leading behavioural research scientist based at Oregon Health and Science University. His simple conceptual formula states that performance can be considered in terms of three specifics: Motivation, Ability and Obstacles. He designed the performance equation, which is:

Performance = (Motivation + Ability) - Obstacles

Where:
Performance is the delivery of a valuable result via human behaviour.

Motivation is linked to receiving recognition for a job well done and receiving regular feedback on performance. At work, someone's motivation will normally come from natural positive consequences in the task, their peers or their supervisor/manager. Motivation tends to be higher when people feel confident, free, and valued. People's past experiences affect their motivation (e.g., their own unique reinforcers), however the local workplace environment will be the primary source of motivation at any given time. Task completion can be motivating, especially when people have a good fit with their task assignments, but not always. Great leaders purposefully 'supply' motivation into the environment where it may not otherwise naturally occur.

Ability is the ability to do the job required. Does the performer have the necessary knowledge and skill level required to do his or her daily tasks? The first step to ensuring ability is selecting people with the right experience and skills for the job. However, after that they will require the right training, information and knowledge. Job ability requirements also change over time, so it is important to ensure that people get ongoing support and coaching. A person's ability also depends on the right people around them being available when they need them and enough time being allocated for each task.

Obstacles or 'The removal of obstacles' involves making sure that people can do their job well, and that their environment is free from safety and health hazards, unnecessary complications, rules or bureaucracy. Work procedures and processes should be lean and straightforward. Communication, including emails and meetings, must be uncomplicated and effective. If there are barriers preventing people from completing simple tasks quickly and easily then high performance is just not possible. High levels of performance occur when frustrations and distractions are low and where people can consistently do what they say they will do.

Performance = (Motivation + Ability) - Obstacles

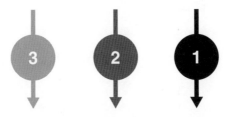

Dr Olson states that the first step (and highest priority) in a performance analysis process is to look at the obstacles that stymie current performance. The second place to focus is the ability of the performers, including the leaders that are presiding over the particular workplace environment. Step three is to look at motivation. It's quite common that once obstacles have been removed and the performer has acquired the necessary skills and time to complete the task, motivation fixes itself.

This is because steps one and two were usually the key elements stopping the performer all along.

Understanding the workplace environment of the performer is paramount in using scientific methods to adapt behaviour. All three components in the performance equation should be analysed from the performer's perspective. Simply put, if the performance isn't occurring then it's because the performer either can't or won't carry out the desired behaviours. This is illustrated below:

Performance = (Motivation + Ability) - Obstacles

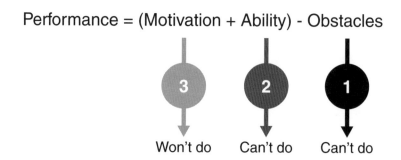

Olson's simple process can be combined with behavioural analysis to change the environment where the performer can achieve their goals as illustrated below:

Performance = (Motivation + Ability) - Obstacles

11.4 Behavioural models – Workplace environment analysis

This section was devised by Bruce Faulkner, a leading behavioural consultant and founder of the BMT Federation.

One reason that it's easy to fall into the too busy trap is that a leader's focus is often in the wrong place. Most organisations focus primarily on results, monthly KPIs, annual accounts, objectives, profits, overhead etc. (illuminated below). These are known as trailing (or lagging) measures, they are 'after the event' results measures, bad, good or exceptional. Once published they are what they are, and no-one can change them. Their opposite numbers, leading measures, tend to comprise behaviours that will one day contribute to the end result. Measuring a balance of leading and trailing indicators is an excellent way of reporting organisational and personal performance. This is covered in the Hollin booklet, *BMT Scorecards.*

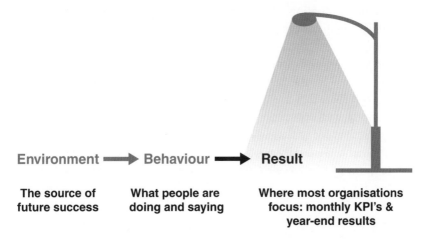

Environment ➡ Behaviour ➡ Result

| **The source of future success** | **What people are doing and saying** | **Where most organisations focus: monthly KPI's & year-end results** |

Behaviours are always driven by the local workplace environment, which includes all the things said and done by all the people within the particular environment. The environment is laced with an abundance of leading measures that can predict the future results. The environment is created primarily by leaders, and all the people within the environment are sensitive to change. Replacing just one person in a team can have a dramatic effect on that environment.

When things go awry, organisations will often attempt to deal with their problems by introducing new policies and procedures. These are usually attempts to narrowly define and constrain behaviours within their organisation in the belief that better results will be delivered by increasing control. This act is commonly insensitive to the context of the performers within their local workplace environments. This 'go to' artless response to problems is a mistake made by leaders who do not understand the value of taking the trouble to analyse their workplace environments before acting (or over-reacting).

The effect of attempts to increase control over the workplace can be catastrophic and is often a major source of disengagement. To illustrate, the people in the organisation currently generate 100% of 'A' and 'B', and then there is a new demand for an additional 100% of 'C'. This demand builds in competing priorities which of course impose the 'addition' rather than 'removal' of obstacles in the performance equation. By asking for 'C', the artless leaders lose the surety and quality of the delivery of 'A' and 'B'.

The artful solution is to observe and analyse the current workplace environment. Use the performance equation to diagnose problems, and design fixes that increase the chances of high performance. Discretionary effort occurs in environments where workers can thrive. Behaviour will always perfectly adapt to its local environment. Generally positive environments carry with them an R+/R- ratio of four to one (four behaviours people perform because they 'want to' for every one where they 'have to'). This key aspect of reinforcement ratio can be measured and the environment adapted accordingly.

It is paramount to harvest the available leading measures in the organisation using simple anonymous surveys. These will quickly reveal the ratio of positive (R+) to negative (R-) reinforcers within the environment (and any apparent punishers for that matter). Regular testing of the workplace environment will provide crucial information regarding performance. High performing teams gather feedback at surprisingly frequent intervals.

People in organisations are usually focused on results (illuminated in graphic below), and often fail to take into account the environment or behaviours when making decisions:

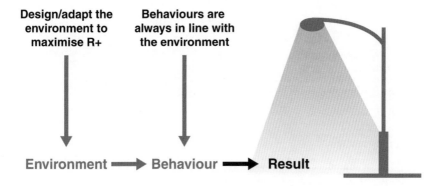

Design/adapt the environment to maximise R+

Behaviours are always in line with the environment

Environment ➡ Behaviour ➡ Result

The graphic below shows where organisations should be focused, i.e. on the analysis of the local environment. The behaviours will always be in line with the environment, and the right behaviours will deliver the desired results. This process is always followed in successful organisations. This is the same caring process that parents follow when creating a safe household for their children.

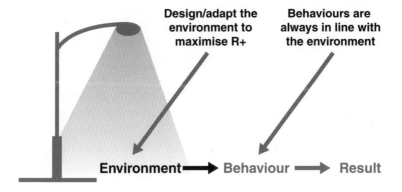

Design/adapt the environment to maximise R+

Behaviours are always in line with the environment

Environment ➡ Behaviour ➡ Result

11.5 Simple places to start fixing *'too busy'*

I urge people to measure something, anything, and find a good friend you can trust to have safe conversations regarding your workplace environment. The key to avoiding any trap is recognising the signs that you are close to the jaws of it, and this is a skill in itself. You can look at your diary at any time and ask the question: Am I spending my time on all the right things? Understand that your inner wimp (from the Hollin book *Ideas for Wimps*) will be lurking so perhaps you could separate things out like this:

1. Stuff completely in my control and of my making
2. Stuff completely in the control of others that I have no choice but to obey
3. Other stuff

I would now find the person you trust and have a discussion about the details in 1, 2, and 3 above. Make a list of your daily behaviours, annotate them 1, 2, or 3 and have a discussion with someone who will be honest with you. You need to be hearing agreement for things you have marked and you also need to be hearing scepticism about the delusional stuff you have in there. If you aren't hearing any scorn, find a better friend.

11.6 Work from home during the week

This is an amazing piece of therapy that works really well. If you can, work from home one day a week, two half days etc. You will discover you get an amazing amount of stuff done, probably mostly tasks but also plenty of wealth-creating stuff too. There is research out there that talks about how much productive work suffers in the office because of the vast array of distractions.

As I look at this magnificent vista here from my office I can reflect how effective for me working from home is. Of course my family have all flown the nest and it's quiet here; I have a comfortable chair in a comfortable room. There is a great Ted Talk by Jason Fried called 'Why work doesn't happen at work,' and it applies to the next section also.

11.7 Recognise the destructive power of self-delusion

Distractions make people feel *too busy*. Someone said to me last week, "My problem is that at any one time I have got 45 unread emails in my in box." I said, "OK, well that will take about 20 minutes to triage, delete the crap, answer the easy ones and decide what needs more thought. Remember though, earlier on today you spent 20 minutes talking about football to the guy over in the kitchen. Perhaps have a long think about whether your perceived busyness is truly a problem or a convenient delusion." Most people can reduce the volume of received emails by walking round and asking people to stop sending the ones they don't want to receive - a couple of well-aimed hours, problem solved.

In a workshop, someone who is a serial complainer of being *too busy* kept looking down at a phone on the chair next to him. I leaned over to see that he was selling stuff on eBay and it was sending bid notifications, two or three per minute!

Transferring responsibility for personal daily behaviours to a PA, secretary or assistant is also a common act. In the old days secretaries typed out letters, managed a hard copy diary, and provided other administrative services to their boss that the boss could not perform themselves. Times have changed, email has superseded letters and online scheduling has taken over from diaries.

We all need a balance of activities in our daily workplace lives, and I quite like answering my own emails, booking my own flights, managing my own diary etc. These activities provide relief to the fully focused stuff (like writing this!). In an average day I would expect to be 'fully focused' for about 2-3 hours. Turning notes and new material into half decent copy is tough brain work, researching takes less concentration as I flit about on the internet, reading is fun and relaxing. A balanced day is a fulfilled, productive, effective and probably a happy day.

11.8 How did I end up here?

Of course if someone has an uninspiring job, it makes the available distractions even more alluring. Perhaps they could say to themselves, "I'll do thirty minutes work and then go and have a chat with someone, another thirty minutes and get a coffee." The bottom line here is, if it's this bad, they could probably get a better job somewhere else; most people I know vastly underestimate their value on the open job market. Don't let a poor job or a poor organisation succour you into thinking that you are less than brilliant. Realise your potential and go somewhere else where they might appreciate you!

11.9 The emergence of the principle of expertise over time

Successful leaders develop and utilise their expertise rather than relying on 'time and effort'. Way too many companies still reward time and effort - first in to the office, last out etc. Presenteeism is very easy strategy for lesser talented people to follow. It is, of course, very easy to measure: "I can see you are here, therefore you must be adding value." This is a massive misnomer. People enthusiastic to show their commitment to a job or project are often reluctant to be seen leaving on time, concerned about the message it sends. This may be a useful strategy when you are new in the job market, but over time it is unsustainable for a healthy work/life balance.

Dr Anders Ericsson, Professor of Psychology at Florida State University is internationally recognized as the leading researcher in the study of expertise and human performance. His renowned paper 'The Role of Deliberate Practice in the Acquisition of Expert Performance' is regarded as a landmark work. His speeches on expertise in sports are particularly interesting.

Ericsson talks about 'deliberate practise'. It's the difference between sitting at the piano and noodling the same few tunes, and actually working to improve your playing skills. There was a saying in my old company about someone who had not realised their potential: "He has been here 20 years but has just done the same 2 years 10 times!"

Professor Dan Ariely talks about an example of a locksmith as a descriptor for what is meant by 'expertise'. His story goes: A man locks himself out of his house and calls a locksmith. The locksmith, who has just started his business, comes to his house and spends about 40 minutes picking the lock on his front door. He lets him back into his house and charges $100, which the man gladly pays. Some years later the man locks himself out again. The same locksmith comes round and has the lock picked in 40 seconds. He charges $100 again but this time the customer objects, as it didn't take any time at all. The customer's paradigm for payment was 'time and effort'. He received his desired result much quicker than last time, but he didn't value the expertise that delivered the quick result as much as he'd valued the time and effort of the first attempt.

Deliberately practicing what you want to be expert at will in time deliver that ambition, and that includes the effective use of time. Your deliberate plan for the week will always beat anything improvised. Over time we can all be expert in time management and look back at those *too busy* days with a shudder and a knowing smile.

Joni Mitchell recounted some time spent with Pablo Picasso. They chatted and as the meeting came to an end he sketched her on his notebook. He handed her the sketch and she said, "Wow, that's amazing and only took you two minutes!" "No," he replied, "That took me 40 years." Forget being *too busy*; developing expertise is the goal, it will ensure that other people stay in touch with you as you get older!

> *"Learning is not attained by chance, it must be sought for with ardour and attended to with diligence."*
>
> Abigail Adams

Appendix A -
Other Hollin publications

All Hollin publications are available at
www.hollin.co.uk/shop

POWER COACHING
By Howard Lees
ISBN number 978-0-9575211-2-4

THE STEPS BEFORE STEP ONE
By Howard Lees
ISBN number 978-0-9563114-9-8

NOTES ON BEHAVIOURAL MANAGEMENT TECHNIQUES
By Howard Lees
ISBN number 978-0-9563114-1-2

HOW TO EMPTY THE TOO HARD BOX
By Howard Lees
ISBN number 978-0-9563114-4-3

HOW TO ESCAPE FROM CLOUD CUCKOO LAND
By Howard Lees
ISBN number 978-0-9563114-8-1

BEHAVIOURAL SAFETY FOR LEADERS
By Howard Lees and Bob Cummins
ISBN number 978-0-9563114-5-0

BMT SCORECARDS
By Howard Lees
ISBN number 978-0-9575211-1-7

IDEAS FOR WIMPS
By Howard Lees
ISBN number 978-0-9563114-6-7

BEHAVIOURAL COACHING
By Howard Lees
ISBN number 978-0-9563114-2-9

Appendix B -
Further recommended reading

I like to read. In fact, I am the guy on the train reading a book while most of the other travellers are frantically trying to get their internet connection restored. These books are all packed with varied wisdom of some kind. There are a number of useful shorter publications you could download from our website should you wish to start with an entrée.
www.hollin.co.uk

1. What Got You Here Won't Get You There - Marshall Goldsmith
2. Turn the Ship Around! - L David Marquet
3. Maverick - Ricardo Semler
4. Why Employees Don't Do What They're Supposed To Do - Ferdinand F. Fournies
5. Bringing Out the Best in People - Aubrey Daniels
6. The Hungry Spirit - Charles Handy
7. Coaching for Improved Work Performance - Ferdinand F. Fournies
8. Performance Management - Aubrey C. Daniels and James E. Daniels
9. The Sin of Wages - William Abernathy
10. Other People's Habits - Aubrey C Daniels
11. The Tipping Point - Malcolm Gladwell
12. Mojo - Marshall Goldsmith
13. Myself and Other More Important Matters - Charles Handy
14. Open Minds - Andy Law
15. Leading Change - John P Kotter
16. The Empowered Manager - Peter Block
17. The 20% Solution - John Cotter
18. Measure of a Leader - Aubrey C. Daniels and James E. Daniels
19. The Elephant and the Flea - Charles Handy
20. How the Mighty Fall - Jim Collins
21. Good to Great - Jim Collins
22. Body Language - Allan Pease
23. Experiment at Work - Andy Law

24. OBM Applied - Manuel Rodriguez, Daniel Sundberg, and Shannon Biagi
25. Yes - Noah Goldstein, Steve Martin and Robert Cialdini
26. The Empty Raincoat - Charles Handy
27. Unlock Behaviors, Unleash Profits - Leslie Braksick
28. Built to Last - Jim Collins and Jerry I. Porras
29. On Writing - Steven King
30. Don't Shoot the Dog - Karen Prior
31. Learning Reinforcement Theory - Fred S. Keller
32. The Seven-Day Weekend - Ricardo Semler
33. The First 90 Days - Michael Watkins
34. How to Deal with Difficult People - Ursula Markham
35. The Leadership Pipeline - Ram Charan, Stephen Drotter and James Noel
36. Understanding Organisations - Charles Handy
37. The Principles of Scientific Management - F.W. Taylor

notes:

notes: